D0518785

Invitation to the Bold of Heart

THE SWISS LIST

DOROTHEE ELMIGER

Invitation to the Bold of Heart

TRANSLATED BY KATY DERBYSHIRE

LONDON NEW YORK CALCUTTA

swiss arts council
prohelvetia

This publication was supported by a grant from
Pro Helvetia, Swiss Arts Council

Seagull Books, 2011

First published as *Einladung an die Waghalsigen*
© DuMont Buchverlag, 2010

English translation © Katy Derbyshire, 2011

First published in English by Seagull Books, 2011

ISBN-13   978 0 8574 2 019 0

British Library Cataloguing-in-Publication Data
A catalogue record for this book is available
from the British Library

Typeset and designed by Seagull Books, Calcutta, India
Printed and bound by Hyam Enterprises, Calcutta, India

What curious events slumber in the foundations of such reports, we can no longer establish with full clarity. That a core of truth lies therein, however, is certain, for in the primeval layers of the earth we find countless curious skeletons and remains of quite outlandish creatures.

Wunder aus aller Welt, VOL. 5

We clambered out from these depths and were on the crest of the hill. A pleasant beech wood girdled the flat area adjacent to the hollow and spread out on both sides of it. Several trees standing there were already withered, others were fading, and next to them were some that were still quite fresh and without presentiment of the approaching fire that was menacing their roots.

In the open area various fissures were smoking, while others had ceased to do so, for the fire had been glimmering some ten years through the old choked tunnels and shafts which honeycomb the hill.

Johann Wolfgang von Goethe,
My Life: Poetry and Truth. Part 2, BK 10.
(Robert R. Heitner trans.)

But away, boys, look about you, and seek for anything that may be useful to us.

Johann David Wyss, Swiss Family Robinson

I for my part was often alone with the books. No one could tell by looking at me.

I got up in the mornings and made coffee. I stood in front of the books. I contemplated them. I drank my coffee and went away.

Later I came back again.

I knew nothing about the books. They had been in the apartment above the police station forever. I did not know who had brought them here, I did not know who they belonged to now, nor who they would belong to later.

I read the reference books and the textbooks. Treatises on mining science, books about shipping, the second volume of *Introduction to History* from the bourgeois revolutions to the present day, an introduction to astronomy, *The Oceans of the World*, two volumes on the birds of Europe and *Alaska–Mexico* (*9148 Miles from Anchorage to Oaxaca*). *The Living Desert, Winston Churchill, The Plant*, Volumes 1 and 2, *The Beauty of America, Islands in the Atlantic. Angers sous l'occupation. Alpine Flight, with 191 Aerial Photographs and a Colour Plate After a Painting by F. Hass. Wunder aus aller Welt*, Volumes 1, 5, 6 and 7.

DOROTHEE ELMIGER

I read at the kitchen table. While Fritzi roamed the
territory, I read. An agreement we had never made.
Sometimes I looked up from the kitchen table at the
very moment she walked past outside, slowly crossing
the country far away. Though she walked slowly, she
once went all the way to St Beinsen. I took my bearings from the pit frames, she said on her return.

I piled the books on the kitchen table. I conducted
research. At some point I discovered tiny flowers in
one of the 191 aerial photographs Walter Mittelholzer
had shot in 1928, flowers I was already familiar with
from *The Plant*, Volume 2. The sixth volume of *Wunder aus aller Welt* explained to me how aeroplanes are
constructed and function. *The Living Desert* was mind-
boggling, and Walter Mittelholzer flew over Mount
Kilimanjaro on 8 January 1930. In Volume 5 of *Wunder aus aller Welt* was a chapter on mining by Hanns
Günther, who also wrote *The Boys' Book of Flying
Machines*. In which: *The pit frames tower above the shafts,
which lead vertically down into the earth.*

I held on to everything worth remembering, giving reports in the evenings. Fritzi listened and added what-
ever else had to be said. I said, for example: Joseph

Conrad on the North Sea pilot: *He mistrusted my youth, my common sense, and my seamanship,* and then Fritzi said she had roamed through dingy weather, reached a peak in the land and felt no astonishment.

We knew little. I did not know why I read the books. Fritzi did not know what had to be said. In the summer we simply imagined at first what it would be like in winter. We'd get lost in the hills due to heavy snowfall!

The lie of this land was unusual, our situation unprecedented; I could not find it in any of the books. At least I could pencil a cross in the atlas above the coal plain, read the time zone we were in. I noted down the longitude and latitude.

Our birthdays too: Fritzi Ramona Stein 17 April, Margarete C. Stein 25 September, Heribert Stein 4 July, Rosa Stein 5 January.

I noted down the names of songs in the form of a list.

The Fire Came Up to My Knee

To the East

Everyone Knows This is Nowhere

Return to Burn

We knew little. They were conspiratorial evenings; we ate hard-boiled eggs and leeks. Preserved tomatoes, turnips and celeriac. We peeled potatoes. Ours was an uproar in the kitchen.

It was not until later that I took a typewriter from the station, took it from the desk by the rear window, took it and carried it up the stairs, while the officers smoked their cigarettes by their cars on the driveway. Officer Schroeder—the son, we would later find out, of Mayor Schroeder—had typed police reports on it.

Like every policeman in this town, Schroeder carried a Model 700 Remington repeating rifle on his back, a tried-and-trusted weapon from the sixties. *Blam blam blam. Ratatata tat. Ka-pow.* In the year 1816, I read, the twenty-three-year-old blacksmith Eliphalet Remington began producing rifles and shotguns. Several years later, the company also commenced production of typewriters. The police in this town possess four red Remington typewriters from the sixties.

Writing entailed considerable difficulties; Officer Schroeder's Remington stood firm on the kitchen table. Countless attempts were made. I wrote:

Fritzi Ramona Stein and I, we are the youth of the town, the only daughters of a police commander and a renegade woman, largely unknown to us.

Our inheritance is an abandoned territory.

Great devastation prevails here, and we do not know how to deal with it.

We have forever been its children.

It is our youth.

We must have come too late.

Though they tell us nothing was better in the old days, and though the police commander and his officers can do nothing but patrol, half-heartedly cite regulations and obey chronology, though our mother has long since set out in solitary, we would have been pleased to have some hints handed down, instructions for actions regarding the future, a handbook for work, for revolutions and the sea. *Lift your skinny fists like antennas to heaven*, it might have said.

Yet any link between the ancestors, possible past events and us, the present youth, has been successfully prevented. Everything has been handed down only in part. It is possible that the police commander in his fervour administers history as well, or it lies fallow in his hands; that's my suspicion. Reports from the past are stored in filing cabinets and card files at the police station. As statistics, as a logical conclusion, as incontrovertible evidence.

Attempts at a chronicle. It was supposed to help us in this mess. I wrote:

Try to be obedient! That is, try to subordinate the events obediently to what is generally acknowledged as history. That is, try to subordinate the events obediently to a chronology, even though the chronology is tantamount to a brazen simplification, plus a relativization and a fundamental renunciation of contradiction, of the formation of non-blood ties and affiliations. Of the sudden emergence of possibility.

Typed later:

On *modern man's position on the past*,

on the significance of the old markings in the territory, pit frames, shaft entrances, railway tracks, piles of rubble. On the significance of the more recent and most recent markings: fissures in the ground, paths to nowhere, subsidence of the earth's surface.

On Joseph Conrad, who once sailed a load of coal across the seven seas and also wrote reflections on youth.

On the writer James Jopek, rather thin and slender of limb. At the age of twenty he is thought to have spent three weeks shovelling coal in a mine for the sake of experience. Shortly afterwards, he joined a collective of young London historians who wrote a book on the British workers' movement.

On the Argentine poet Alfonsina Storni, who threw herself into the sea at La Perla beach in October 1938.

The territory gives birth only to fear and horror!
It gobbles up rabbits, mice and ferrets in one bite!

In the end, I simply tried to explain myself.

This is the tale of a town in the process of disappearing. After nothing other than a fire broke out in the ground decades ago, and continues to burn in the tunnels.

It shall also tell of the few houses now left standing in the deserted land, of their inhabitants male and female.

The description of the lives of the Stein sisters. Where and in what form they enter this world, what they see, learn, experience and endure in it.

The youth read books and search for a river. The youth think of meeting at the river in the future. They cannot recall the time before the fire, but they try nonetheless. Journeys are undertaken. A horse joins them.

There is nothing mysterious about the entire story, although it may cause confusion in places, unsettling those with weak nerves as life often does. Unfortunately, this cannot be prevented.

It shall be told by the Stein sisters, whereby Margarete Stein has a stronger tendency towards storytelling while Fritzi Stein is often occupied with studies in the field.

FLORIDA

It was early evening. Two police officers were leaning against the outside wall downstairs, talking quietly. I spent a long time watching them.

That evening I had read about the river for the first time.

My friends in Missouri advised me to bring tools to build canoes and go down this river to the Pacific.

The river unfolded visibly before me. Its name was Buenaventura. It flowed calm and wide, yet not without its perils. At times it seemed rough to me; barely sprung from the eastern flank of the mountains, it crossed southern heat, subtropical regions, Florida.

I was alone. Fritzi was out roaming. Our father H. Stein was downstairs in the police station. I had not yet told Fritzi about the river. I ate a slice of bread, then sat back down at the table.

Two padres and an old cartographer had discovered the river on their 1776 expedition. It was an early autumn day and the cartographer probably walked stooped over, as he had a stomachache. The three of them held a show of hands to agree on a name. The cartographer hastily jotted down the river and its location in his notes and they continued on their way.

Along with the reports in the books I had found a map from 1823 on which a river with the name Buenaventura flowed into a lake. In widely spaced inked letters to the left were the words *UNEXPLORED TERRITORY*.

The officers were still there when I looked out of the window. I couldn't see them, the darkness had grown too great, but I heard their voices.

The western boundaries of this lake are unknown.

I adjusted the beam of light from the desk lamp. On further expeditions years later they had charted the unexplored territory. They had missed the river, then failed to find it again, then looked too far to the south. They suspected it further eastwards, they believed it to be in the north, they doubted its existence—*buena ventura*.

In 1844, J. C. Le-Mont definitively ruled out the river's existence. His geographical surveying expedition had failed to find it either. When he made his report to the country's president, the latter called him young and spoke of the *impulsiveness of young men*.

Fritzi entered the kitchen late in the evening. She hung her anorak over the back of my chair. And still the torrent flowed wide before my eyes. I said only this: According to my own calculations, the river Buenaventura still flowed straight through this territory 240 years ago.

Fritzi nodded: Then we must look for it.

That evening:

I climbed on my motorcycle and drove around the town. With me drove a great unrest. The town was dark, a light still burning on Elisabeth Korn's first floor, but that too was soon out of view. I left the town behind me. *I sought the Buenaventura long and anxiously on my journey southward.* Once, unexpectedly, the motorcycle leapt over a railway sleeper, then everything was as it had been.

I recall: I rode far, almost all the way to Usten. Near Usten, they said, the archaeologist Norma J. was digging for fossils in a riverbed. Shortly before Usten, fear took hold of me.

On my late return as I pushed the motorcycle into the garage: Officer Heller sitting alone in the common room, playing with a jackknife. A golden engraving: *Heller*.

Heller, have you ever heard tell of a great river by the name of Buenaventura—a great river, they say, that virtually tore at its banks at times, and its banks were populated by rare creatures. It flowed through this territory, its bed was here.

I recall: Heller, absolving his monthly shooting practice.

I pushed the kitchen table out of the back corner forward to the light. I drank a coffee there. Were the spatial conditions significant for my research? Who had sat here in the dark corner? The maid. The worker after his shift, silent with weariness. And who sat at the window?

Sometimes the mine boss paid an unexpected visit. He was served a better piece of meat to be on the safe side.

I pushed the table back away from the window a little. What was forgotten lay in the dark corner. Fritzi sat down mutely with me; her alarm clock had been ringing for several hours. Her hair stood up in all directions. In silence, the two of us watched what they called the sky here, and what had once been the land beneath it and now merely sprawled. At some distance, three pit frames stood unmoving in the landscape. The steel cables still ran taut over the cable sheaves into the ground. Railway tracks sunk deep into the earth led away from the shafts. The pit frames were the only reference points the land offered. (And the hills? And the houses and the roads?)

The northern coalfield recalled only itself: the men's cable-rides to the depths, inscribing their own time periods on the land.

The rims of my fingernails were black with coal dust. Even if this territory were to be abandoned in the end, I would take it away with me.

Fritzi spoke cautiously about the untenable landscape:

For a long time, she said, I have been trying to comprehend the landscape here. She said, I look at the pit frames rising to the sky, and I look at the railway lines running deeper and deeper into the ground because they're sinking and sinking, I look at the sky, because the sky might also be symptomatic, the sky is also part of this landscape. I count, she said, I count the colours; my vocabulary is exhausted after brown, olive and black, and when I think about it those are all the colours there are here. I look at the few houses standing in the landscape, at random distances from one another. Stubborn and alone, they perpetuate the names of their streets and have lost all context. Formerly aligned in neat rows, the houses stand in the expanses of endless streets, kept from collapsing by high piles of bricks on either side.

She said, the land is lying prone; it's not working any more. The landscape has been shut down and no one goes down the shafts any more. I try to imagine the landscape, the plain. I practice a neutral gaze—I try to view things with no emotion. I call myself an observer and count the breaches in the landscape.

She said, I place myself in the land and look for the smallest common distance to the things around me. I speak their names and remember the names they used to have.

They used to call a birdcage an aviary.

That is how Fritzi spoke about the landscape, at first hand. She was wearing a pair of our mother's old jogging pants, I saw. I put a cup of coffee on the table for her.

Regarding the river:

Police Officer Henrik was one of the fatter ones, his limbs bloated, his fingers grubbing through the files. He spread historical maps out in front of us.

Of course he had recognized us as the youth of the town, who resided in the apartment above his workplace. As the daughters of his superior H. Stein, who made him patrol the territory for hours on end.

No, he said. No river in the territory. No river visible. We stood facing each other, Fritzi stroking her index finger along the barrel of the Remington that lay on the desk. No river in the territory, she said slowly.

Windmills?

Or supermarkets?

Tower blocks?

Grain stores?

Lofts?

Stables?

Farmsteads?

A cinema?

Bridgeheads?

Funicular railways?

Tram stations?

Bus stations?

Subway stations?

Racetracks?

Universities?

Libraries?

Canteens?

Public houses?

Mountain guesthouses?

Sights?

Historical buildings?

Carwash facilities?

Golf courses?

Ski lifts?

Boat hires?

Contact points?

Hospitals?

Post offices?

Bakeries?

Butchers' shops?

Confectioners?

Dairies?

Discos?

Factories?

Industrial plants?

Carpenter's shops?

Metalworker's shops?

Banks?

Officer Henrik shook his head and slammed his hand down on the map.

F/2202167

In the nights that followed I dreamt of the Mekong. The Mekong grew wider and wider as time passed by. In its midst rocked a small transport ship, its freight two cages of hens. At the rudder sat a woman in a hat. Once darkness had broken, when the heat grew even clearer, I heard people's voices calling back and forth, calling from one bank to the other until deep in the night.

Morning came, and I wrote on a sheet of paper:

In search of a river.

Oh buena ventura!

The procedure: extensive research in the territory and in the books on the territory's past and present. Interrogation of those present. Possibly archaeological excavations.

Then I stayed in bed and thought of the animals in the Mekong Delta. Little monkeys clung tightly to the tree trunks, the fish were swimming their paths, a giant catfish passed just below the surface and a snow crane flew past.

One day I went down the stairs and peered through the glazed door. The police officers, they sat there so indifferently and noted everything casually in their files.

Our father was watering an orchid while talking on the phone.

I would start with our father, I thought, with Heribert Stein, police commander by profession, born on the fourth of July. With the father first, then the mother, who gave birth to me after all, the grandparents and so on in succession over time. Would I then get to the Buenaventura? What course did history take?

One day I stood outside in the car park and listened to the pebbles crunching under my soles.

One day I fired up the bath boiler. Then I sat on the edge of the bathtub and touched one tile after another with my feet.

But! I thought, family ties have nothing to do with the matter. *When we weigh anchor and put to sea* no father will help us, *only our companions*.

Then I plunged into the water I had run into the bath.

Fritzi entered the bathroom toward midday, as I was still lying there. She was carrying books beneath one arm.

Now and again, she said, I find signs with specialist terminology outside on a post or a strut. Technical features, maximum load, On/Off, Furnace I, Furnace II, Stop, 1 Amp., Warning, Beware! Here was once: a mine.

These words, said Fritzi, are still suspended above the landscape, though they have long since left the true events of the former time behind them.

She placed the books she had brought with her on the stool by the bathtub. She ran a hand through her hair in front of the mirror, as if carrying the books had been a great effort for her.

Thereupon I began to read again. I looked for the words Fritzi spoke of. They were contained in each of the books, in mining science contexts:

Colliery

Conveyor machine

Pithead frame

Schematic cross-section

Pithead frame

Washroom

Damps

Safety lamp

Cable winch

At the seam, a collier

Later electric locomotive

Cage

Winding inset

Coal yard

I continued all day long.

At times among the books I found myself repeating the words out loud. I did not know quite how to deal with them; what was a collier, for heaven's sake! Yet I nevertheless believed I understood what they actually concerned and why they automatically brought me further words, from earlier days at the kitchen table (strike and sabotage, Berlin, Señor Buenaventura Durruti—a syndicalist and the son of a railway worker).

The words, said Fritzi that afternoon when she poked her head around the door, already contain what we are trying tirelessly to find and repeat. She laughed.

Later I dozed. The water plashed faintly, the fire in the boiler long burnt out.

'Let us leap into the sea,' cried Fritz, 'and swim to the shore.'

'Very well for you,' cried Ernest, 'who can swim; but we should all be drowned. Would it not be better to construct a raft and go all together?'

'That might do,' added I, 'if we were strong enough for such a work, and if a raft was not always so dangerous a conveyance. But away, boys, look about you, and seek for anything that may be useful to us.'

When I awoke again I climbed out of the tub. Last thing that day: I noted with clammy fingers that Buenaventura Durruti's sister bore the same name as our mother. The water flowed towards the outflow in a tiny maelstrom.

Coal seam fires move quickly and stealthily along the tunnels. They undermine the territory, ravaging it.

For some time now, former woodland had been bulging, piling up at a great distance on the margins of the coal district, cracking from the heat.

The next day, Fritzi Ramona Stein took the path to St Beinsen, in search of the river. Raised her eyes now and then, then gazed back down at the ground, that dry ground. I took my bearings from the pit frames, she said on her return. We had long since forfeited the points of the compass.

I carried my sextant on my back, in a leather case.

She took her bearings from the pit frames, I wrote that evening, and:

The reason for these writings, these statements and declarations, the reason too for all elaborate calls out across the land and deep down into its shafts, for all these future consolations, considerations and under-takings, is the search for the missing river.

I wrote:

We are calm. Yet there is a feeling, aching in our shoulders and pulling at our necks, making our jaws tremble. Soon we shall want to speak aloud. Ought we perhaps to forbid ourselves this feeling? Does it make us weaker?

No, it will perhaps create a commitment!

This commitment will not be based on our mutual fear of losing security. That is why we are writing this report on Schroeder's typewriter, neither to maintain order nor to prevent confusion. No orderly confirmation of the old familiar present, no entertaining remarks about our situation in which we have ostensibly settled ourselves so well, like Officer Schroeder behind his desk. (At this, Fritzi called through the open kitchen door, Stop! Stop this early evening entertainment, this evening entertainment, this entertainment in general. Entertainment hurts my eyes, it breaks my back just below my neck, I've had enough of it, my entire life so far has been weighed down by entertainment, entertainment is a deep ditch in the underground of the land, filled up over the years with animal corpses.)

Instead, we are defiantly documenting the confusion and the great lack that opens up under cover of official security; a valley broad and bare. That is the valley of this story.

Hello, I said. Hello, who are you?

'My name is Gerste, Erika Gerste. I am the former and final librarian of the local libraries. I left behind a number of books when I moved away nineteen years ago. I've been thinking of the books and hoping to find them again. Perhaps at the printing plant.'

Ms Gerste. Which books are you thinking of?

'I'm thinking of an anthology on the subject of repetition, a handwritten early sketch of the Communist Party Manifesto and nine treatises on moving bodies of water.'

So these books are why you've come back?

'Yes. I came to the border of the territory by train, to Oberfeldstadt. I wanted to take a taxi from Oberfeldstadt, but taxis are banned in the northern coal district. So I took a bicycle and rode it along the country roads.'

When you talk about repetition—do you mean memory too?

'It . . . well, I remember the weather that passed over the two towers of the printing plant, just as it is now suspended motionless above them, as you can see, and is sinking lower over the towers day by day. It is possible that there was a bell in one of the towers back then.

A woman stood at the stairs to the printing press with a pile of books in her hands. At the rear exit, a woman loaded the new edition of the *Morning News* onto a truck, using a forklift. The typesetters were on the ground floor.

Three apprentices stood on the southern tower of the printing plant and scattered flyers into the hinterland, freshly printed with twenty-five questions. It . . . it is possible that one of them knocked against the bell with his elbow.

But the woman with the books stood at the stairs to the printing plant, and now she cleared her throat and waved, a brief movement of her hand.'

That woman, that was you, Ms Gerste, wasn't it?

'Yes, yes, it was me.'

And do you perhaps remember a river in the northern coal district?

'Oh dear, Ms Stein. I've grown old now. All these questions are tiring me out. But . . . I . . . in my memory I do sometimes sit in the library and look up from a book and gaze out of the window— at the afternoon light reflected in a broad stream far out there. But—

you know these books, young lady, the books . . . Perhaps it was only a river from a book. Although I'd once have sworn—'

Thursday, 4 p.m.:

It is stormy; the present wind speed is high. The weather is good in Weber Valley, but here: drainage winds, storm clouds descend unexpectedly into a trough and upon us.

But in spite of all the variety and commotion of the day I still could not find any rest.

I kept myself busy by staring out of the window.

Empty beer cans rolled out from under the seats as Fritzi took a turning and immediately swerved to avoid a deep fissure in the middle of the road. A sudden speed took hold of us in the low land. I wound the window down; we were a blue point on a line on a plane.

Down on the edge of town near the old swimming pool, a stretch of road had caved in. The officers had blocked it off with red tape. Fritzi stopped the car. We stayed in our seats.

The land was just as silent as it sounded behind the car windows. I was exhausted by the movement we had undertaken across it and by its unshakable paralysis. A raised hunting hide stood far away on the edge of a field.

I cast a glance at Fritzi.

It was very simple, she said, I tore out a wire under the steering wheel like in the movies and held it against another wire. The engine started instantly. Really very simple, she said, scratching her head in amazement.

One day, Fritzi would lie awake on the back seat of this car, far away from here.

One day, we would load everything we had into the car. Blankets, clothes and the books, the coffee machine and the coffee cups, a reading lamp, a crate of beer and that kind of thing.

In the glove compartment were a roadmap and old cassettes. We shouldn't take driving all too seriously, said Fritzi, it is only a very private pleasure. I inserted one of the cassettes into the stereo; the loudspeakers crackled.

Yes, I said.

That evening we drove off again, following the police patrols around town. Along the way: a windmill. Fritzi said: That windmill—

I did not know what to answer either. To be quite honest, I thought of Don Quixote. We drove behind the patrol across a field, another raised hide at its edge. Machines.

I understood very little here; some of it frightened me.

What's this, what is this? (It is time gone by.) Fritzi stopped the car on a field that was burnt and now savannah yellow.

There once was a land in a state of abandonment, etc. It was abandoned, it had been abandoned, it must itself have abandoned us. It was so extremely vast. And had it always been that way?

The town that produced me, Fritzi and me, is situated in the northern coal district, postal code 17921 (no longer valid). Here was once woodland.

I made further notes on the territory and its geography, in the hope of coming across the old riverbed at some point:

Size: The entire territory has an area of 97,103 sq. km, running 294 km north to south, extending 466 km wide from east to west. 5,043 sq. km are bodies of water. I drew a pencil line beneath the words *bodies of water*. The land is criss-crossed by anthracite deposits, divided into four main coal districts named after the points of the compass.

The highest elevation in the land is a hilltop 979 metres above sea level.

The highest elevation in the land is a hilltop 979 metres above sea level. The average height is 345 metres. Downs, deciduous forests, wooded elevations: the land was once woodland. There are no conspicuous mountains to be found. The sea lies far distant to the south.

Population: The territory once had 7,440,561 inhabitants.

Economy: grain, potato and turnip cultivation; animal husbandry; mechanical engineering; precision instrument production; coal mining.

Particularly in the early twentieth century, coal was mined diligently in what is referred to as the northern coal district. The shafts were closed in the 1960s due to fires.

Aha, aha, ah.

And who had dug the first shaft? What was his name, what on earth were their names, what were their feelings, what was their creed, those men who went down the shafts?

Wherever we enter the realm of coal, we encounter the same picture all over the world.

The days passed tight-lipped. Fritzi's alarm clock rang for hours, and Fritzi said she needed an unprecedented amount of sleep. Sometimes she wore spectacles now, which we'd found on a workbench in the abandoned printing plant.

Fritzi was lying in bed as I entered her room. My back ached, my feet were cold. I believe, I said, our undertaking is doomed to fail. We will never find the river. Fritzi raised her head, gazing at me through narrowed eyes. She threw a pillow at me. Keep looking, you weakling! she called. Then her head fell back onto the bed.

As I wrote, I thought: It is obviously presumptuous to write. I am far too young. And at the same time: Later is too late, it is now, always *now*, and *at all cost*.

I spent my days in this small kitchen, typing on Schroeder's typewriter. I listened to the news on the radio and the traffic reports from distant towns and valleys. As I wrote, I thought that I would never experience anything in this kitchen, and at the same time that there was nothing to experience outside either, nothing worth mentioning. And the days and the hours passed me by, moving past the window with outrageous regularity, as I sat in the kitchen quite calm and untouched by it all.

They had declared invalid all manner of efforts for improvement. They had declared that there was nothing more to do. The fires could not be extinguished. No need to repair the damage. The River B. had never existed either.

The police commander declared with a smile that we should come to terms with the situation.

Only the televisions were operating, transmitting all manner of things, *CashTV*, *EveningQuiz*, *StockInfo*, *BodyTalk*, *MotorSport*, so that nobody here forgot they were, in fact, still in this world.

And the actual symbol of the coalmines, the pit frames, tower above the shafts, which lead vertically down into the earth.

The police officers had bought stocks and shares some years ago, and Heller, the youngest officer, had treated himself to a new police car out of his own funds. These were their only statements to date concerning the future.

At last I found a few useful pieces of information on the shelves, wedged between the books. A few photographs: 4 December 1908. *150 people homeless following a fire.* Standing under a bare tree, in front of it two horses. In the background swathes of smoke and, as if snow were lying on the ground: piles of rubble and ash. Fire laid by the mining company, to gain access to the coal seam directly beneath? Letters, notes: 12 May 1902: strike. 3 October 1902: *122 striking miners force strike-breakers in a railway carriage emblazoned* L. A. Rilken Mining Company *to turn back.*

One photograph shows the L. A. Rilken mine in its entirety in the year 1880. Photographer: G. Schwarzer, Wildenstadt.

Dug-out ground in the year 1963. Mammoth Coal Company. Tiny digging machines in the foreground.

Erik Danz, aged eleven, sitting on the huge fan over the ventilation shaft, 1959. Son of the local brass band's first trumpeter, Karl Danz.

One M. Schroeder, father of the aforementioned officer, in a newspaper article. He is frail, eighty years of
age, wearing large spectacles on a starkly bent nose.
The caption: *Now in his late eighties, M. Schroeder has
never left our town. He took on the office of mayor five years
ago. Asked why he stayed despite the fire, he replies: This is
the only home I've ever known.*

I too: the only land I had ever known. Now it was the
land of the deserted—we were born deserters in these
parts, bereft of our senses.

GRAND ERG DU BILMA

Oh!

They withheld certain things from us! They left us to wait alone. They covered up events. They ridiculed all efforts. They failed to tell us our mothers' professions. They instructed us to be content. They lulled us into a false sense of security. They threatened us with its loss. They feigned liberty. They did not speak to us about the shortcomings. They left us in the dark regarding the events of the past centuries. They told us only isolated incidents to appease us. They tested the tactics of de-escalation on us. They rode roughshod over us on police horses.

It was on the thirtieth day of our explorations when a long summer began. The officers ducked down at the sight of the heat. Fritzi made tea and poured it into bottles that she piled in the refrigerator, lay sleeping in the bathtub for days.

It was a town, only desert. Where was the echo sounder to measure our sea depths?

I thought of the sea, which was here too in the beginning and first became dry land and then became coal, before they dug the mines and drilled the tunnels, undermining the entire region and calling it the northern coal district, before the cable sheaves revolved upon the pit frames and there was day and night and sky and ground and underground.

The sea, which was here first and thereupon withdrew, but left behind a river. A favourable wind.

An old wood grew into the bathroom, made up of memories. That summer we watched as it gradually spread out along the walls. Our heads lowered, we stayed in place, and the longer the summer lasted the more restlessly Fritzi slept in the bathtub that contained the last sea.

In the middle of the summer I got up and stepped outside.

They had never told us our mother's profession.

Our father H. Stein and Officer Bussig were sitting in one of the police cars, Schroeder and Dünckel drinking on the back seat. Bussig solving number puzzles. Sweat ran in dark streaks down his neck, despite the air conditioning. There was a curious calm, the offices abandoned. Perhaps the other officers had lain down sheepishly and secretly in the shade beneath the pit frames. Perhaps that was the great capitulation. I knocked on the window of the driver's door. No, Heribert Stein gestured, the window can't be opened, that would disrupt the great air-circulation cycle. I sat down in the shade of the car and waited.

Our mother was like Hemingway, the police commander had said one day. She roamed the territory, smoking cigarettes and writing on a typewriter about the things that she saw. Like Hemingway, she always went away and came back again, and she was safe all alone. Between birth and departure was a single event worth remembering, the police commander had said: our mother had her hair cut short by Elisabeth Korn. She came back from a roam of the territory with her hair cut short and smoked a cigarette in the car park outside the station, so that all the officers could see: the wife of Police Commander H. Stein has her hair cut short like a man now, and soon afterwards she departed.

That great earnestness, the police commander had said one day, that she used to carry around with her! It's better that she's gone. That woman does not get on with people.

47

It was on the thirtieth day of our explorations when I sat in the shade of the car.

The Grand Erg Occidental in Africa, the Grand Erg Oriental, the great Erg of Bilma, Igidi Erg, Rebiana Erg, the deserts *Erg Shesh, Fesan*, the deserts *Gapawa, Hamada du Draa, Hamada el-Hamra, Kalahari* made the branches of the old boxwood droop low to the ground, the great deserts of *Kamaturi* made my boat rot at its lowest point, I was thirsty at the sight of them, the animals had already perished, towards the end seeking liquid even in their own stomachs. The great deserts of *Karakum, Kysylkum, Lakamari, Makteir, Masagyr*, the deserts *Moritabi, Mujunkum, Trarza* carved their way, leaving a number of traces on the Alps towards the end, *Uaran*.

I pursued certain considerations. So far we had been able to find out nothing about our mother. She had left this place, after all. Had driven away in her car. We could do the same, I thought.

I dreamt of a horse, the officers plunging their knives into its neck. Then they took their knives and twisted them in the horse's neck and twisted great holes into the creature. Dünckel knelt on the horse's head—its eyes leaping out darkly—to make the creature hold still at last.

I dreamt of a day in autumn 1977, and the officers, nodding off at the wheel, drove head over heels into a chasm.

Later I got up and sat down at the kitchen table and waited there for hours. Far above my head, the fan rattled in a circle. Up there,

far above my head, the machine circled in the air. Up there—

and on the table lay a bread knife. Had I a child I'd call it Ohnesorg: Carefree.

At night the only light was that of the television in the station. The officers sat around it, and their noises and the film music rose quietly through the floorboards into the room where we sat and waited.

We drank the officers' beer. In this town no points of the compass were recognized, the smoke hid the path of the sun. And thus time was lost.

Fritzi opened the beer bottles with a lighter. Sitting at that window meant being closest to this landscape, it meant waiting for nothing to change, it meant holding out motionless like an animal, a lizard.

At least, I said, we're drinking the beer we've appropriated from the station.

Fritzi nodded. Appropriated, she said.

Now and then the generator went off in the station and the noises fell silent. Then the officers walked up and down outside the house or patrolled the territory in their cars. The headlights did not reach far. At some points in the land they had drilled black vent tubes into the ground, from which slim grey columns of smoke ascended. Pit frames stood motionless, their precise position impossible to establish. Only in our exotic nature did we become allies of the landscape. Fritzi got up. Her hair tumbled over her eyes, she stretched her arms to the sky and turned in a circle, she stretched her arms out horizontally. In the darkness I sometimes saw her silhouette or her eyes, a reflection on her hair, above all I felt the air. It was a secret dance. It was an audacious movement, distancing itself from this land.

I felt no other anxiety but to pass safely across the intervening desert to the banks of the Buenaventura.

And then I stood up and walked away, the officers briefly raising their eyes and nodding as I crossed the room and left the house. The caps of the beer bottles jangled in my pocket. That was all.

I mounted my motorcycle and drove through the town again. I thought about driving away, thought about an attempt to go away, leave this place. I thought I would go one day, drive to the crossroads and then onwards.

On the southern shore of what appeared to be the bay could be traced the gleaming line where entered another large stream; and again the Buenaventura rose up in our minds.

I would reach the river flowing silently like the Mekong, as if it had always been there. Yet I was not certain. My suitcase stood next to the bed. I had not opened it for a long time, for this was not the journey. The journey would not begin until later.

In 1980, a number of canaries still perched in their cages in Jacques Malz's hairdressing salon. Once Malz had sold the birds to the miners. As the carbon monoxide concentration in the region was constantly rising due to the mine fires and the entire stock of carbon monoxide detectors was sold out, Christine Aicher, a twenty-eight-year-old mother of four, put on her coat and went to the hairdresser's. She named the canary Fred.

In preparation for the explorations, I turned to the old maps. The river was only noted approximately, its course only hinted at.

But around the town there once lay hundreds of tiny towns, as I discovered on the old maps. A handful of houses and a few shaft entrances, most likely all owned by the respective local mining company. Exactly, said Fritzi, in every town everything belonged to the mine: the police, for example, were mine police and mainly and primarily protected the coal from the residents. I saw that one of these towns was called Wärgl.

When I reached Wärgl: tired now, I parked my motorcycle next to a garage. I saw that Wärgl was not far from Ansburg, and a light mist floated freely in space at medium height. Beforehand, I had almost overlooked a car coming towards me from the right at a turn-off.

There was no one there. In a few strides, I walked around Wärgl's few buildings, weeds growing in all their nooks and crannies, the rooms empty. There was an electrical hum above the place. I sat down on the steps that had once led to the mining company's administration building. All that was left was the sign, hanging on two wires: *L. A. Rilken Mining Company*. What had I expected of this place? Wärgl! Like a slim church tower, a transformer station loomed into the sky at one end of the town.

At the garage I came across a man getting out of the car that had come towards me from the right beforehand. It was Robert Selbig. A former miner.

'There was a conveyor belt, connected to a second conveyor belt by a funnel, that was all. I sat above the funnel and stared down, watched the coal moving along eight hours a day. In the event of a jam I stopped the first conveyor belt. Sometimes I fell asleep. Sometimes I only woke up when the coal had already piled up above the cabin where I sat. Sometimes I fell asleep. Sometimes I woke up. Sometimes I despaired of it all. I was virtually always alone. Sometimes a conveyor belt caught fire. Sometimes I jemmied mansized stones back down with a crowbar.'

What did you do after that, Mr Selbig, after you had left the mine?

'I retrained as a salesman.'

Are you happy now, Mr Selbig?

'I've actually only ever been interested in music.'

Have you ever heard of a river by the name of Buenaventura?

'No. Although the name does summon up vague memories. There are very many things I have almost forgotten. Sometimes they come back to me: the revolt of the fishermen of Santa Barbara, shipping across flooded open-cast mines on bright days, the songs my wife once sang in a rowing boat.'

On these days during the long summer I read a great deal about shipping, and an image came to me of a ship in this landscape, a stranded vehicle like a huge and breathing creature. The sails fluttered in the wind.

I wanted to eat fish: to be precise, I was thinking of rollmops. I wanted to lay pickled herrings on a board and spread them with mustard. Gherkins, onions, capers. Juniper berries, cloves, pepper to taste.

I sat down at the kitchen table early in the morning, before my usual time, and put forward the suggestion to our father, Heribert Stein, who was spreading a bread roll with potted meat. Fritzi sat attentively in the darker corner.

No, said H. Stein, fish was not taken into account in the budgeting for this town, which is in a state of emergency.

His hands lay flat on the tabletop. Fritzi brushed her hair out of her eyes. We ought to start every day with a piece of fish, I said, it seems to me this would be a good omen. Fritzi nodded: We'll pickle herring and then wrap it around pieces of gherkin, stabbed through with tiny skewers.

Is there anything more to add? asked H. Stein. Nothing to add, I said. H. Stein stood up.

One day I said as well: How can it be that this large swathe of land does not produce at least a few potatoes?

Police Commander H. Stein narrowed his eyes, as if measuring the size of the land, and said: That's the way it is. How many more times are you going ask?

(Perhaps a few more times.)

And when the houses began collapsing, when the houses burned down and the old trees outside the houses that had been there for centuries, and then the cars suddenly sank into crevasses, and the car tyres gradually melted into the tar, swathes of land subsided, when the land fell in, when smoke and steam masked vision for weeks—

Well, said H. Stein. And what else? Fritzi fell silent.

The book *On Circumventing or Removing Individual Sections of the Existing Construction* by Hirsch and Elm had been published in Turin in 1951. It was hidden in the first-aid kit in the car. Hirsch and Elm wore hats on the book cover, two young Canadians who'd shipped over to Italy at the age of twenty-four and twenty-seven. They allegedly studied Statics and Dynamics at Turin University, according to the jacket copy, and later built.

the great arched bridge at Hölltobel,

several steel-framework railway bridges in Canada,

and in particular, according to the jacket copy,

the Rose Blixt Overpass, the New Turnpike Bridge,

and in Europe

the Hotzentötz Bridge,

the Weberschlucht Bridge,

and an arched bridge made of fieldstones, at an unnamed location

(Italy?):

Ponte sul fiume Bonaventura, according to the jacket copy.

I pored over the maps of Italy I found in the flat for a
River Bonaventura. Then perhaps, or so I thought, it
might all have been a misunderstanding; instead of in
Italy, J. C. Le-Mont might have entered the name of
the river on the wrong map.

I drank coffee and roamed to and fro in the kitchen,
thinking. I picked up the book and gazed at the picture of Hirsch and Elm on the back cover. Hirsch was
tapping two fingers to the brim of his hat, wearing a
pale shirt. In the background Elm was leaning against
a wall in Turin, laughing.

Ponte sul fiume Bonaventura.

When I asked H. Stein about Hirsch and Elm that day,
he confiscated the book with a police-approved arm
lock and threw it on a smouldering pile of plywood
behind the station.

Fritzi shrugged. Elvis Hirsch?

H. Stein poked the pile of plywood with one foot until
the book *On Circumventing or Removing Individual Sections of the Existing Construction* caught fire.

A bridge is a man-made construction for the purpose of cross-ing flowing or still water. Canyons, valleys and heavily used roads, lowlands, ravines and railway tracks can also be crossed by means of bridges. Only when the clear width be-tween the bridge piles is at least two metres does the construc-tion constitute a bridge.

Why don't you call Erika Gerste? said Fritzi.

Ms Gerste says all these questions make her very tired, I replied. Then I called her anyway.

Ms Gerste, I said into the mouthpiece—

'Elvis Hirsch wore a flat cap and carried a machine in a transport case, the latter labelled with the letters *B.o.M.Q.* Eric Elm carried nothing, but was kind enough to explain the meaning of the handwritten let-ters on the transport case, namely *Bureau of Mining Questions*, along with *site security, geopolitical and geostrategic matters*, while he connected a needle sensor to the machine. These gentlemen—'

Elm and Hirsch.

'. . . Elm and Hirsch, who had travelled from Oberfeldstadt, positioned certain buttons and the machine
came to life. We met at the gas station . . . down south
of the crossroads. As there was still a large amount of
fuel contained in the underground storage tank, peri-
odical testing of the ground temperature was essen-
tial, Elm explained. He inserted the sensor into the
ground while Hirsch knelt before the machine.

These gentlemen . . . er, well . . . these gentlemen
were engineers, bridge constructors. But then, if I
remember their words rightly, they had been banned
from exercising their profession. Because they . . . people had suspected they were communists. Yes, it was
in Italy that . . . so then there was a ban on their communist . . . er, bridges. That was why, as far as I
know, they had taken a job in the Bureau of Mining
Questions—'

LES *RECHERCHES MINIÈRES* AU SAHARA

I roamed through the Coal District, walking step by step, thinking of Ms Gerste. The smoke rising from the black pipes crept into my eyes. I no longer knew where I stood. The wind raced above me in the sky.

LES *RECHERCHES MINIÈRES* AU SAHARA

I roamed, walking step by step, and it was the coal district that surrounded me.

I was all alone. I had to say it aloud once, but only once. I said it to myself and to the bushes, their black branches brushing against my legs.

Nobody contradicted me.

Then I knew it was the poisonous gases making me tired unawares, but I thought too: It's not the poisonous gases, it's the land, as I lay down with my legs outstretched. My head pointed towards the pit frames, one leg far away and the other towards home. I lay like that and saw the pebbles close up and the earth by my face,

63

AU SAHARA

Life, I thought, seems to be a spectacle in which I have no part. The words thought themselves slowly now.

I am almost a blind spot, I thought, closing my eyes and then becoming invisible. It seemed that way at any rate, as I lay like that on the earth, above me the territory and the starry sky.

The winds and the usual horizon. The ghosts.

One more time I heard a sound, saw a police car driving slowly by. Officer Dünckel looked over at me out of the window. Then the car accelerated and drove away. Nobody helped me to get up. Nobody's helping me, I thought, and my arms were too heavy to lift.

I was very tired, and then I fell asleep.

During the days of the summer I took geological and geographical findings from the filing cabinets.

Beneath the town lies one of the largest anthracite deposits in the land, by the name of the Mammoth Vein.

Beneath the town, I read, the four main veins Buck, Sevenfoot, Knievel and Mammoth are nested like four bowls. The lowest is Buck, the uppermost is Mammoth, and between each and every vein are a hundred metres of stone. At the southern end of the town, the coal deposits end at the hills and begin again on the other side of them, where the little town of St Beinsen is (Fritzi once walked all the way to St Beinsen, taking her bearings from the pit frames). In the north of the town the veins extend far into the unruly landscape.

The fire began in the vein by the name of Buck, in the south of the town, not far from the outermost houses, where

the hay in a rick caught light late one evening and, driven by a strong wind, eventually burned its way down to the coal seams via tree roots and fissures.

In the filing cabinets I also found transcriptions of scientific reports on the fire in the mines.

For instance August M. Ray, a scientist in the service of the Swiss Mining Bureau, once said: Mine fires move quickly forwards, upwards and downwards, provided sufficient air is available. The heat forms the vanguard, driving the water out of the coal in advance so that the fire burns well. It is as simple as that. Fires move through old tunnels, making the mine constructions unsafe and weak. The result: collapses that often extend all the way to the surface.

I went down the stairs and knocked at the door.

Officer Bussig opened up. His shirt hung crumpled from his chest. He smelt of sweat. I entered and began my questioning. Officer Bussig, I said, it is now well known that human hands laid the—

Officer Bussig ran a hand across his sternum. Young vandals, he said, juvenile traitors, adolescent excesses—the swine. Excessive violence against their place of birth, tedium, hormonal disorders, destructive behaviour. Disturbed!

Officer Bussig was sweating. Next to him sat Officer Heller, loading empty cartridge cases. He nodded. *Seventeen-year-old Eduard Pitt fell into a mine fire when the earth suddenly opened up*, and perished.

To H. Stein, standing in the back room admiring himself in the mirror, I said: Was it not the case that there
were a total of nine hollows, in which—

Concerning the fire specifically, interrupted H. Stein,
there were a total of nine hollows in all corners of the
town, where the townspeople deposited their waste.
Possible openings that might have connected directly
to the tunnels had been carefully closed. Possible fires
in these waste disposal sites could never be ruled out,
but were combated conscientiously.

The midwife Elisabeth K. rode past the station on a
bicycle. She had aided my birth too with her skilful
hands. I called out her name.

Concerning the fire specifically she said: Police officers set fire to the rubbish regularly on the Wednesday
before Easter. That was the method ordered by the
town council for dealing with the nine waste disposal
hollows. The black smoke fell in tiny particles on
our heads. The men of the volunteer fire brigade extinguished the nine fires late in the evening on each
occasion. Possible openings to the old underground
tunnels are probable, Margarete Stein.

I watched her hands slowly coiling around the
handlebars. And the river? I asked. Buenaventura?

Elisabeth mounted her bicycle and rode away. Her chin-length hair blew in the wind.

Of course she had recognized me instantly.

On that same day, I looked for a long time at a loose photograph I had found between the pages of *Islands in the Atlantic*. Girls in white frilly dresses with daisies in their hair, their hands folded in front of their ribcages, with the caption: *Albina Solani on the way to the Church of St. Ignatius*. Awaiting them there: their first Holy Communion.

A land captivating through its broad and formless scope. No landmarks, no milestones here when I sought an echo.

Fritzi, O Saviour. Fritzi Ramona Stein, born—

> I, Fritzi Stein, was born into an April like
> every other April after it and like all the
> months of the year. Slowly they dragged
> themselves across the land. They roamed the
> steppes as invalids, through the desert, the
> tundra, what do I know, as in a war or after a
> war, these units. All of them were unknown,
> they were disconsolate, and time went slowly
> away with them.

And I, M. C. Stein, born on the 25th of September. It
was a dark, storm-blowing late summer day. Far away,
clouds piled up and then moved on. And they piled
up and moved on with the smoke, and the smoke rose
high in the sky.

> It was a similar day, that day of a new start in
> search of the river. The clouds piled up, and
> I watched that day bringing night anew.

I filled up a sports bag with bread and tinned food,
and Fritzi sang a song,

> O Saviour, rend open the heavens, hasten downwards, downwards from heaven, O God, pour dew down from heaven, flow downwards, O Saviour, in the dew. Ye clouds, break and rain down now, ye clouds, break and rain down now, break, break, break and rain down.

I added a few books to the pile. Soon we'd be setting off now, in search of the river once more. We'd take opposite directions with the same goal. I pressed the car keys into Fritzi's hand. Thunder-headed, we faced each other. Now get out of here, I said, thunder-head. And she sang on mockingly,

> Earth, break out, break out, O earth, make all mountains and valleys so green, O earth, bring forth this flower here, O Saviour spring out of the earth. That is what I sang.

The geo-scientist Marie-Louise Steinhauer wrote in the compendium *On the Great Deserts*: In many cases, the formation of deserts (desertification) is directly linked to unsuitable cultivation of the areas concerned, with false irrigation methods often used.

In China, the desert expands further every year, the city of Beijing battling sandstorms.

Outside the Hotel Bellagio in the desert city of Las Vegas is an eight-hectare artificial lake. Water fountains leap to the sky to the tunes of *Ecstasy of Gold*, *Viva Las Vegas* and *Hey, Big Spender*.

The Aral Sea was previously populated by catfish and sturgeon. On its banks slept goats, wolves, antelopes and mice. Today, the old seaside promenades lie abandoned in the desert.

Fritzi took the sports bag and I carried the backpack. The officers had no idea. They were leaning against the wall, laughing stupidly. Above them as always that sky of coal. It was a calm night, that night, favourable for all types of plans, I thought as I drove off. A quiet nod to Fritzi, who drove alongside me for a while and then soon took a broad curve and disappeared.

Margarete carried the backpack and I took the sports bag. I was born into an April. It seems to me to have been a strange affair: our mother lying on a folding bed in the police-station sick bay. The officers in the next room turning the television up louder, embarrassed, staring over the edge of the screen into the expanses of the early evening and listening to her scream, this wife of the police commander, and then unceremoniously give birth to her child. While the police commander no doubt stands alongside and frowns, and a slight desperation comes over him, only a single time, when he sees the bloody head of the child with its slight covering of hair appear between his wife's thighs and it's far too large, oh far too large, because the child grew for

too long in her womb and grew so large, oh
so large and heavy.

Fritzi had slept in, unlike myself. As Elisabeth the
midwife grabs hold still young and undaunted, grabs
hold with her bare hands and lifts the child out of the
woman, before it can tear the woman's body apart
with its large head. It seems to me to have been our
mother's second-last decision, to give birth to that
child Fritzi into that April, before her apparently last
decision to leave the town one November.

Perhaps she too steered her car straight across
the fields, as I am doing now. Perhaps she too
took her bearings only from the wind and the
weather, like sea captains, and began driving
blindly straight ahead,

thinking: just straight ahead. My mother was a
Ukrainian diplomat, my mother robbed a casino in
Reno, she studied geography in Russia, in Naples she
sang with the partisans, she caught three hundred buf-
falo with her lasso and tore the hearts out of their
chests with her bare hands, and the hearts, still warm,
gave off steam in the cool autumn air.

Perhaps she too had steered her car straight across the fields that November. Perhaps she had glanced at the rear-view mirror now and then, but all had remained dark behind her, all had let itself be left behind without a word. That is: the house, the flat above the station, inside it a police commander and two daughters, one of them me.

There were no maps, no more accurate maps for the northern coal district. It was absent on all the plans, it was one large absence, so to speak, the course of the roads long since slightly shifted, hills diminished, towns abolished.

Slowly, I followed a country road, taking hours, for the fissures were dangerous. At their base accumulated what had been left over the years, to start with perhaps a fawn that stumbled in now and then, regularly cattle, small creatures and rubbish, remnants of former inhabitants of the area. I was alone that night, thinking of Fritzi for brief moments, hoping she was sleeping, hoping she was awake and restless like I was now.

As I drove that way I was more alone than before, although the road remained the same one. I waited for the birds—I had long been thinking about how it would be to see birds at last, flying low circles, tracing synchronous lines just above the car's hood with their wings, in the air above my head, jays. Sparrow, sparrow.

My mother was Hemingway; I may well be Don Quixote. And while Fritzi drove further north, towards Hasseldorf, I drove to the demarcation line,

where, in the softer climate of a more southern latitude, our horses might find grass to sustain them, and ourselves be sheltered from the rigors of winter, and from the inhospitable desert.

At seven in the evening I saw houses for the first time, emerging from the mist on the edge of the road as silent relief. Here too were pit frames in the immediate vicinity, here too all was quiet, but also lights, a gas station with two illuminated gas pumps, a drinks store, an ironmonger.

The houses outside Hasseldorf were long and low and stood on wheels or on axles with their wheels missing, and they were inhabited. Light shone wanly through the windows, draped additionally with sheets. Cars parked on the edge of the road, trashcans on the patches of grass between the houses, a broken lawnmower lying by a garage, lying by car tyres.

This is the continuation, I thought, a first continuation, and I've made it this far. Everything seemed as abandoned as in the place where I was and where I came from.

The evening at seven is a creature ducking down!

I sat down on the kerb outside the gas station and ate bread, thinking: Hemingway. Rooms to let, said a sign. In the darkness I saw the outlines of trailers, all lay quiet, now and then blue television light.

The evening at seven!

The gas station attendant Ernst Thal said he lived here in the peat district: All the rooms are to let. After closing time, he mounted the motorcycle behind me. I thought: What is the earth like here? Tell me, what is it like with peat, where the earth is black and everything else too? What is it like in the place where you come from, as you do? How do you become when you come from a place where the earth is black and simply empty, flat, low in vegetation? In the tailwind, the gas station attendant said: In the peat you get older and older, you age in tribute to the levels and the layers.

Fritzi! Behind the house, several hundred yards up the hill, begin the woods, said Ernst Thal as he flipped three eggs in the frying pan. The woods are the border to the empty district. This is where the watershed is, where one time zone begins, where the last one ends.

The demarcation line.

As he spoke he grew restless. The thought of the woods now standing in the dark, though they would be clearly visible behind the house again in the morning, suddenly seemed to haunt him.

They are a kind of riverside forest. He put two plates on the table. The ground is largely under water, flora and fauna intact, and they say bears walk the woods. He smiled. Let's eat, he said.

Hasseldorf has been abandoned as well. All that remains is a trailer park. The trailers are long with low roofs, painted white or red with white windowsills, dark on the inside, dark wood panelling, small windows, swamp-green carpeting, soft. On the roofs small satellite dishes, trembling slightly when the early autumn wind blows hard.

Fritzi, fir green is not to be confused with the green of the spruce, deciduous green, evergreen—periwinkle. I tramped through the woods in the early morning, thin branches brushing my face, threatening to scratch my chin, stroking their leaves across my hair. I was looking for the riverbed. I roamed through the thicket along the border, past the forest hut with blind windows, I followed trails and beaten tracks and went further and further through the riverside woods. The gas station attendant Ernst Thal, who was letting me a room, sat at the window drinking coffee as I stepped out of the woods, overstepped the demarcation line and shook clumps of earth from my shoes. He was wearing a cardigan and reading a book, like a man aged before his time and not a mere twenty-five years old. I nodded at him, a little out of breath, my mind still in the woods with the spruces and jays and with the cast-off antlers of the roe deer.

The room in the gables sloped low above me as I slept. A woodland creature howled in the woods. Through the skylight, a slice of light fell at times precisely into the corner of the room, something I had no memory of whatsoever. It reminded me of nothing, just like the knot holes in the wall, the cold windowpanes on which my fingerprints slowly vanished after I had pressed my hand to the glass.

Then Ernst Thal sat in his kitchen and wrote. He seemed to want to overcome all obstructions that came his way with his left hand, which held his pencil, pressing the words deeper and deeper into the paper. Perhaps that was the reason for the exhaustion that overcame him, hours after he had closed his notebook, an exhausted desperation that seemed to plunge upon him, gradually appropriating his body.

I sat down at the table.

> A house like this, Margarete, is built with a screwdriver. You stretch plastic sheets over the windows in winter, and over the space between the floor of the house and the ground, otherwise small creatures crawl underneath and die, lying there until their cadavers are entirely decomposed.

> They came back here. When their houses collapsed, when the cracks first ran right across the facades and then the houses collapsed entirely, they stayed here, set up the trailers instead of their houses. Got themselves a dog. Stretched sheets of plastic over the windows.

> The only thing they built again was the church, and again and once again. Hoisted it

up from the ground with the last of their strength.

Ernst plucked elderberries from their stalks, his hands stained red. Your house is in a semi-shaded nook, I said. He rested his head on his hands.

The house was in the immediate vicinity of the forest/ empty district demarcation line, Fritzi, it had a peaked roof, and in the kitchen was a table, at which we sat and preserved the berries, which didn't quite work out. We had done something wrong and the red, viscous mass sloshed over the edge of the saucepan. Ernst lay down exhausted on the sofa, his whole body breathing in and out.

In the immediate vicinity of the demarcation line was the house, in which we read. He liked the sentence: *But the Robber displayed a lion's heart*.

Periwinkle shone towards me and I followed its trail. The periwinkle loves semi-shaded places, so I had read in *The Plant*, Volume 1. I walked through the woods, climbing over stones and cords of roots. I bent to pass below a branch, dead leaves making it increasingly difficult to find my bearings, settling doggedly over all paths.

> The way was further than we thought. Days of driving lay ahead of me. A forest, a trailer park, an unobstructed view for long stretches. I lost sight of the coal district here, I forgot so quickly. They told me the territory was lost, they told me it was a waste of time and effort even trying for the sake of it, the territory was lost, the land was exhausted and they were too.

I found Ernst Thal with his body exhausted lying on the bed, in an armchair, on the bench outside the house. It's not the writing, it's the land, he said and smiled thinly, drawing a blanket over his shoulders.

Surrounded by lions and tigers, by panthers and buffalos, by antelopes, stags and boars, I walked upon the mountain-side and dwelt in the forest.

> Margarete, all I found was this: Between a wood and a trailer park flowed a rivulet, in it mainly and primarily a single bird. It perched on a branch that bent crookedly out of the

water. Its head moved sometimes for brief
moments, then it held still again as before.

Fritzi, in this semi-shaded house of nooks there was a
thin, brown-bound book, on its spine in golden letters
Bruckner and *Pains of Youth*. Ernst Thal was lying
on the bench outside the house in pain when I picked
it up. Am I going to die now? he said and laughed.
The youth was in pain, but its sickness was not its
own fault.

I read in the book about the pains of youth. Ernst
Thal's mother had left it behind in her house. *It's wrong
to desert.* And *You think I care about your moral principles*?
These lines spoke of the youth of 1928.

> Desertion was my territory. I deserted straight
> across the fields following my mother's exam-
> ple, and only made it to Hasseldorf. No trace
> of a river.

I found bed and board here in this house by the
woods. I asked about a river; they had heard talk.

> And is there a reason why there is no history
> here, only the coal district and the line that I

drew within it, from its northern centre to its
outer perimeter? Now I'm driving back again.

Now I'm driving back again. The gas station attendant
Ernst Thal is asleep on the bench outside the house.

In Belkenburg too, a mine fire had broken out a good thirty years ago. It ignited in a hollow filled with mattresses, chairs, clothing and easily flammable trash that a hurricane had once deposited there.

Shortly before my departure Ernst Thal and I made a list of possible sentences.

There is a history and a story, but O Lord we do not know it.

Where are the mothers?

There is elderberry juice in the refrigerator.

What has happened since 1928?

What is happening now?

Forest means beyond.

Can the youth and the territory be equated at this moment?

By the spruce and the jays! By the cast-off antlers of the roe deer, where is the river?

This is it, gentlemen, the Dragon has come!

Report on the explorations in the territory, on the time spent in Hasseldorf and close to the demarcation line.

Wind rumbled over the station, a radio playing somewhere on my return. I entered the house with the backpack over my shoulder.

Everything was just as before.

Fritzi was sitting in the kitchen. I heard her voice already: Report on the situation in Hasseldorf and surrounding area, she said. There had been nothing to find there. Everyone had made their getaway. A pair of sneakers under a park bench, collapsed lopsidedly. A few trashcans from which the foxes had helped themselves. And after my return, she said, I watched television with the officers. Now I know what's happening in other places, in other parts. There is rather a lot happening and it has nothing to do with me, says the newsreader and say the officers. But recently there have been jackdaws flying here. Jackdaws are the seagulls of the inland.

The gas station attendant Ernst Thal also spoke of a certain Buenaventura Durruti, I remembered at that moment.

There was no other option but to begin the search over and over again. Our animal bodies paced restlessly to and fro between the various rooms of the flat.

My chronometers and barometer, which before rode so safely, were now in constant danger. The trip of a mule might destroy the whole.

Fritzi disappeared into the bathtub while I stood at the kitchen window, watching Officers Henrik, Dünckel and Schroeder in the car park, smoking cigarillos. Heller vacuumed the dirt out of his car.

I sat down in the dark corner. Even here in the desert, I heard the faint rush of the river. It had to pass nearby, at some point between St Beinsen and Wärgl, Hasseldorf, Ansburg and the demarcation line. Some rivers disappear and only appear again at a different point, the gas station attendant Ernst Thal had said. They enter an underground karst country and winding caves through a sinkhole, a ponor. Then they flow into the Chinese Sea. They flow in a southwesterly direction, past a campsite. They re-emerge just past the airport.

Perhaps our mother Rosa Stein had seen the river one last time before it vanished into the ground, or had she driven over a bridge near where it flowed to the surface?

Rosa Stein, the Ukrainian diplomat.

I made coffee, hearing the water flow out of the bath-tub. I inserted a new sheet of paper into the typewriter.

Not only was Rosa Stein an adventurer, she was also a big-game hunter and a high-seas fisherwoman. In Russia she studied engineering and revolutions, in Reno she robbed a casino and bought herself a freighter with the cash.

Fritzi tied her laces in the hallway. Personally, she called through the doorway, I suspect our mother is in River Forest, Illinois.

Rosa Stein was born on the 5th of January in a house with a veranda and a cranberry bush out front in River Forest, Illinois, only a few blocks away from 339 North Oak Park Avenue in Oak Park, Illinois, where Ernest Hemingway had been born before her and a train from Chicago ran over the railway bridge and the house in River Forest leaned over in its lee.

She was the daughter of two Anglo-Saxon Protestants in the operetta business, who held out poorly in the land of America. Our mother, in contrast, succumbed to the spirit of the gold-diggers and the desperados. By night she imagined Butch Cassidy, that dirty thief, swinging onto the passing Union Pacific wagons to escape Pinkerton's detectives.

Butch Cassidy allegedly passed away, said Fritzi, in the Bolivian mining village of San Vicente in 1908, shortly after his last great coup, a heist on the safe of the A. Mining Company near Tupiza.

By night, then, the young Rosa Stein thought of Cassidy and soon set out. Took the train and went to Chicago, before coming here and giving birth to her children, which Cassidy would never have done.

What Cassidy would never have done:

Changed his horse for another. Betrayed the Sundance Kid. Changed sides.

He would never have gone over to the police.

Fritzi laughed. She drank a cup of coffee standing up. I want to go to Usten today, she said, and talk to the archaeologist Norma J., who is digging for fossils there in a riverbed. She picked up her anorak from the chair.

Rosa Stein, a young Scotswoman, ship's cook on the Red Kraken at the age of twenty-one, sailed with Pirate Kid Red-Leg and thirty-five buccaneers, bound further and further eastwards all the way to China, where she entered the opium trade, which eventually brought her to America, where she settled, not by choice, to give birth on dry land to the children conceived from her brand new fiancé.

Rosa Stein, born in the town in question and never having left it, having experienced the last few years in the unharmed and prosperous territory before the underground fire began to burn and she celebrated her fifth birthday, before her father vanished into a cleft in the earth shortly later and then her mother, before she placed herself in the hands of Police Commander Heribert Stein, who seemed safe and strong. Before she gave birth to her children in this inhospitable district.

Rosa Stein was Hemingway.

One September evening I visited Elisabeth Korn.
Dark, heavy swathes of cloth hung before the windows in all the rooms. I followed her up and down
stairs through the house and the rooms, which were
all cleared out. Picture frames and nails had left traces
on the walls. The floor crunched slightly under our
feet. Books were piled along the walls in high towers
and long rows, books upon books, very many books,
all of which Elisabeth must have read over the years.

Why did you cover the windows? I asked, and Elisabeth left my side. Where is Fritzi? she asked, and I
said: In Usten, and I shook my head when she asked
if our father knew.

I looked at the books in Elisabeth's living room. *Noble
Deeds of Woman*; or, *Examples of Female Courage and
Virtue*.

Fritzi is looking for traces of a river in Usten, I said,
and she wants to speak to the archaeologist Norma J.,
who has pitched her tent there. Elisabeth folded her
arms, looking old quite suddenly.

The river, she said, Buenaventura, Bonaventura,
favourable wind, or good adventure—I have heard of
it. My mother—or was it the former librarian, Ms

Gerste?—told me it often happened that, yes, that rivers disappear, through a sinkhole, a ponor. Withdraw underground. So I have heard, she said.

I left.

Not for good though, she called after me as I went down the stairs. Sometimes for decades, she called. Sometimes for a very long time, not for good though, she called, at some point they emerge again.

Elisabeth Korn's husband Hansjakob had lived in a hut by the printing plant for a long time before his death, I heard. The involuntary job as a policeman in the territory had been bad for his heart, I was told. However, Elisabeth Korn had been found several times sleeping on the floor of that same hut with her three sheep, I heard tell.

After Hansjakob's death Elisabeth Korn had taken down every board of the hut one by one and burned them in a fiery abyss, they said.

In Moscow, the crosses are removed from the towers of the Kremlin.

The first thing that would have interested me is whether there were horses in Africa. Did Walter Mittelholzer see a horse on his flight over Mount Kilimanjaro? Did he see old stallions standing in the Savannah? Was there a horse in the great desert? Did Haile Selassie ride up to the Swiss aeronautical pioneer on a young mare, when he delivered his Fokker with his own two hands?

J. C. Le-Mont believed in the river's existence, and his plan was to reach it before the dead of winter and hibernate upon it.

Here, they took the horses down the mines, where they stayed until the end of their days, which were not really days any more, merely imagined days in the never-ending night.

In the books I discovered Bataille, an old mine horse. *Bataille was the oldest horse in the mine*, it said. And for eleven long years Bataille walked the tunnels, sometimes grazing the rough walls with his nostrils, his eyes staring through the darkness like those of a beast of prey.

Fritzi found a horse in Usten. It must have strayed onto the hill through the bushes. She took it by the halter, which was brittle and almost colourless, and led it away from Usten and down from the hill to the cross-roads where a sheet of paper fluttered on the traffic light and frightened the horse.

I pointed the name Bataille out to her. She said it was a name that probably suited this last horse in the deserts of Africa.

I thought of the stumbling mule.

Perhaps all I had to do was write long enough about the horse's hair, and then everything important would have been said.

No, no! cried Fritzi.

No, no! cried Fritzi and said, of course we shall speak of this white horse's hair. And we shall speak too of the little pebbles on the way from here to Hasseldorf. We shall speak of the time just before the night and of nightly times, of the changing of the light as the day goes by, of the signs of autumn approaching. We shall speak of the pieces of paper we find in our pockets in the evenings, and of the old paths in the territory.

Yes! We shall speak of the old paths, the last bushes on their margins. Of the little birch tree with its round leaves down at the edge of town behind the swimming pool. Of the fine veins of the round leaves of the little birch tree. Of the houses and the huts.

But it's not enough. Margarete! It's not enough, do you hear me!

We have to think of the white horse's hair in the future as well. We have to speak of the time just after waking up, of the changing of the light for the better as a day goes by, of the signs of the next day approaching, a day which will be as we wish it. Of a flamingo and a sparrow and a snow crane circling above the territory. Of the feet of the albatross and of Hemingway's daughters. Of circles of friends. Of books that end

99

with fishermen rising up and ships casting anchor. Of the performing bear catapulting himself through the top of the circus tent from a trampoline. Of the wild-cat secretly building a nest in the bushes. We have to meet in the warmest room of the house! We have to maintain correctly that this state is not the last. We must not believe that things are incontrovertible!

We must talk now as well of the unknown paths in the territory, and of the old familiar paths now forgotten. Above all we must talk of the river, the River Bue-naventura, until we find it. That day will come!

From the archaeological site near Usten, Norma Jackson, aged thirty-one, also told of the sinkhole. A ponor, said Fritzi, that's what she called it. And that's how it is, Norma Jackson had pronounced, rivers sometimes emerge back to daylight, after decades, hundreds of years, and flow in their old beds once again.

Because: a ponor can usually only accommodate part of the water, only when the amount of water is visibly reduced can it swallow it all,

do you understand?

Temporarily invisible does not mean inexistent, you see. Only a few are still aware of what a river once meant for this territory, must mean now and can mean one day. The territory now needs the river badly. The water could extinguish large parts of the mine fire. But listen, although there's no proof, I am certain our mothers, great grandmothers, foremothers, ancestors, all the far-back generations once walked by this river as it flowed onwards at speed. And again and again, I am certain, the courageous and the greatly dissatisfied leapt onto small boats they had built, inviting everyone to a great regatta or simply rowing away to other shores, tossing red carnations to the people on the banks. And the people put them in their buttonholes and walked around like that for weeks.

It was because of these troublemakers, these hotheads, loudmouths, hooligans! malcontents! that the police erased them from the files—the rivers.

Nothing is supposed to remind us of them.

From Norma Jackson, aged thirty-one, Fritzi had brought back a telephone number. Project and Construction Bureau Kohle, Berlin, she had written on the margins of an old newspaper. Reinhard Fleischer, mining engineer. Hel-lo, hello, I called excitedly into the telephone. Heavy clouds romped and stomped outside the kitchen window.

Mr Fleischer, what dangers did mining entail?

'For example firedamp explosions. Miners use the term damps for the gases occurring in the mine, aside from breathable air. I quote: *Firedamps are mixtures of air and flammable gases, especially methane, plus hydrogen and heavy hydrocarbons. They can be kindled by a spark, coming about for example through striking steel against stone*. And in the old days it was often the miners' naked lamps that sparked off the mixture of air and methane. Canaries are of use for toxic but not flammable gases.'

Mr Fleischer, are there further dangers in the mine?

'Of course. Further dangers of mining are—to quote from my own reports: *Rock fall, rock burst, gas escapes, collapses of entire pits and coal dust explosions. Constructing mines can cause mining damage, a consequence of the rock movements prompted by the cavities.*'

Have you ever heard of the previous existence of a river in the territory of the northern coal district?

'Er, according to my documents mainly anthracite coal was mined in the northern coal district up until the sixties. A fire that consequently broke out made the area almost entirely unusable. There is nothing about a river here. However, Ms Stein, the administration of the older documents is completely out of my hands. I have no access to them.

Generally speaking, the sea would then come into play, which was there where you are in the beginning and then became dry land and then coal. Later they dug the mines and drilled the tunnels, honeycombing the entire region and calling it the northern coal district.'

So you don't rule out that a river once flowed here?

'Heaven forbid! It is quite possible that a river existed at that or a later point in time, a relic of the former sea. But please bear in mind, Ms Stein—that is not the official position on the matter.'

Thank you very much, Mr Fleischer, I said breathlessly into the telephone long after he had hung up. I remembered the windmill we had passed one evening in an open field. The rear lights of the patrol car had just disappeared in the dark. The officers were probably unaware of this windmill's existence, even though it lay on their daily route. That was the way for us in all matters. Without doubt, we remembered certain things, but in this territory it was the police who were always right for now.

LAS VEGAS

I was in Usten, I also entered Hasseldorf, I visited
Belkenburg, viewed Hinterzell, St. Beinsen, Wildenstadt, I walked through Unterdorf, drove once around
Wärgl. I saw the edges of the woods, I heard a bird's
call, from far away the humming of the transformer
station in Wärgl, I thought of the Mekong, of the
Nile, the Amazon, the Yangtze, the Po and the Missis-
sippi. I searched for the Buenaventura.

Above my head flew an albatross, yet it did not land.

I walked all the roads in the south and followed the
paths to the north. I roamed to the east and of course
to the west. Fritzi too had walked these streets, she had
rode out ahead of me on the horse Bataille, she had run
after me, had crossed my path at regular intervals. We
met by chance on the edges of the woods, in the deep-
est valleys, at small standing waters, ponds, puddles and
pools, we met below the pit frames and at the great
mine ventilator, we rendezvoused on the savannah-
yellow field, for we were in search of the river.

And the light rose and fell, and the days passed with
quiet footfalls. Once it was summer, then came the
autumn, and soon it would be winter.

At times I called Ernst Thal. He seemed to be tired from his work at the gas station. I suffer a defeat every time, he said, the last remaining residents of this place are rough-hewn people, they'd like to poke my eyes out with their car keys. The more silent I am, the more impatient they are. I'm a bandit.

In the hallways of their trailers, in the ruins of their houses, they cross themselves before their hundred crucifixes of private property, he said. I answered that the police officers look upon us with scorn here.

Fritzi was walking outside with the horse on a loose rope. A horse has an unerring instinct for water, she had said, its nostrils tremble and it raises its head in excitement towards the horizon.

Where the albatross flew.

I drew the movements of a horse walking fast in ten separate sketches.

The horse in motion

In the late autumn I suffered a shortness of breath. I sat down in the dark corner of the kitchen and tried to be sensible. Perhaps my thoughts had hastened after the future for too long. In my chest I felt a painful rattle: a large clockwork mechanism seemed to be moving in there. I had almost finished reading the books.

While Fritzi roamed the territory, I read. Fritzi was out and about. No river in the territory. No river in the territory. No river visible. Had I once said the word albatross? I threw a glance at Fritzi. The land has 7,440,561 inhabitants.

Fritzi nodded.

Fritzi stood up. Fritzi sat attentively in the darker corner. Fritzi brushed her hair out of her eyes. Fritzi, O Saviour. I pressed the car keys into Fritzi's hand.

Fritzi sat in the kitchen.

Fritzi tied her laces in the hallway.

Fritzi laughed.

Rosa Stein was Hemingway.

Fritzi found a horse in Usten.

Fritzi nodded.

It was already not getting as light as it once had. The winter already lay above the most distant spot I could see. You zealot, I scolded myself. Did you once say the word Buenaventura?

Then I walked slowly down the stairs. Officer Heller was sitting at his desk.

Out of interest, I said, I'd like to ask a few questions,

Question 434/35: Do you ever lend money or objects to your friends? Why/why not?

I said, and the first question is:

What is your relationship to money, Officer Heller? And the second question: Is it not astounding, or rather annoying, or has it not always been clear, that even in the end when everything would be over—as is the case here and now—precisely this thing would go on lasting: namely, money? The third question: I'm so tired, Officer Heller. Are you content?

Yes, said Officer Heller, there's no love without money.

Without money I wouldn't have been able to purchase my car.

Though they say being poor isn't necessarily a bad thing, an understated watch emphasizes your masculinity.

In April of last year, two men and a woman appeared in the territory. They introduced themselves as representatives of a company, not stating its name. They would, they said, buy up the land on which the town was built and erect a new town to the south, if they obtained in return the right to mine the remaining coal beneath the town.

In April of last year, two men and a woman descended slowly from the heavens on golden parachutes, not setting their shoes on the dirt as they landed.

After talking to Officer Heller I stepped outside into the evening. Perhaps I had been wrong. The clockwork in my ribcage was still turning.

I sat down on a stone with my back to the house. There were only a few days to go before the first snowfall put a final stop to our search.

That evening, before the frost, the officers measured their plots of land. They pushed surveyor's wheels ahead of them on long sticks. In silence, they moved apart in a star shape from a common starting point, then pivoted almost simultaneously—right, right, right. The perambulators whirred quietly.

Yes, the measurement fell in their favour. After all, there was no one else there any more.

Fritzi and the white horse Bataille returned at that moment. Write it down! said Fritzi, write it down quickly please before I forget it. There are different methods of surveying land. The first step is to decide on a measuring tool. But the choice of the tool itself requires careful consideration of course, as it will, may or should be closely linked to the desired results of the survey. Whereby the actual matter of interest is the motivation behind such a land measurement. The first step therefore is to consider the purpose and intention, before then taking up the tools in question to measure the land in one way or another. Finally, the insights into the land thus gained can be interpreted in differing ways.

The possible measurement tools include the measurement tape, the yardstick (ruler) or metre stick and the modern perambulator (surveyor's wheel). Measurement by string or by thumb is also possible in principle. However, it is difficult in this location because of the lack of reference points in the landscape.

Despite this wide variety of options, astoundingly only a single method has been used.

Fritzi narrowed her eyes and squinted far away, to where Officer Henrik was struggling with his perambulator before a hill. It's all about rescuing private property at the very last moment from its descent into the tunnels, she said. She spat on the ground.

The officers hammered sharpened posts into the pallid ground and linked them into fences. They hammered on the flat ends of the sharpened posts until late at night and then wrapped wires around the posts around their land. Schroeder plot, Henrik plot, Heller, Bussig, Stein, Dünckel. The frost stood at their backs and at ours too, as shown by the clock now bumping against my sternum, and the beating of the hammers that would not end, all for nothing.

In the early morning Officer Heller fitted his fence with a remote-controlled gate. The River Buenaventura! It had almost vanished from my sight.

In the morning the hammers lay on the car park outside the station. The white horse Bataille stood nearby.

In times of earlier land surveys, the step was often used as a length measurement, said Fritzi. The resulting difficulties are immediately obvious, and modern measurement tools only appear to correct them.

I whistled on two fingers to the horse, but it did not move. Fritzi gave a satisfied laugh.

Old hammers, she said then, known as miner's hammers. Just below the hole for the head, the seal is branded into the wood, you see: *L. A. Rilken* and sometimes only *L. A. R.* and sometimes illegible. The miners had taken these hammers down with them, down underground. And did you know, she asked, that they all left a pick and a hammer in the tunnels, on the last day they went down there?

That means 4,557 picks and hammers, or 200,000, perhaps even 851,300 picks and hammers are now scattered below ground throughout the territory. 851,300 tiny dots of remembrance of the miners, of work, of that time: the great heat, the cramped seams, the raising and the cutting of wages, their cutting again, the fire, the damps, the horses and the birds.

The miner's picks were loose on their handles, as these often had to be replaced. In the meantime the wood might have swollen or burnt, but those 851,300 picks and 851,300 hammers are still there, said Fritzi. Bataille shifted his weight.

O yes, I knew the winters fleetingly. They came again and again, but one day soon they would stay.

To that the gas station attendant Ernst Thal said over the telephone: Sometimes I can't help thinking of war.

When we threw the hammers in the shafts, six days before the winter, a large hare ran past and vanished underground.

Fritzi shrugged on her coat and turned around. As she walked away she sang a song.

The hammer of my mother
Oh yes the hammer
Ye-e-e-s yes oh yes the hammer
Soon it will be
Of use to me again
The hammer of my mother

I searched for the echo, not only in the abandoned shafts into which I called.

There came to us forty-one editions of the newspaper for miners by the name of *A Woodpecker Flew over the Shaft*. The poet Peter Wassermann had sent them to us, although we were absolutely unacquainted: To the sons and daughters in the territory, grandsons and grand-daughters, he had addressed the box of newspapers.

The paper of the oldest copies was discoloured; they were almost a hundred years old, others younger than our father, from the period shortly before the fire. Someone had made notes on some of the pages in pencil and underlined certain sentences, most likely Peter Wassermann:

Presumed river

he had written at one point in the margins. Another time he had underlined *Rosa Luxemburg* and a few sentences of Friedrich Engels. In edition number 53 he had underlined the word *tomorrow* a total of eleven times on all pages. On the title page of number 70 he had drawn ballpoint moustaches on all seventeen miners in one photograph.

On one occasion he wrote several lines about a wood-pecker next to the title.

When the woodpecker flies by in the evening,
we shall gather in the morrow.

Fritzi gazed thoughtfully over the rim of a water jug. We shall gather in the morrow, she said slowly, shall we gather in the morrow with the horse Bataille, a hammer and a pick in remembrance?

Dear Mr Peter Wassermann, wrote Fritzi, sitting in front of the water jug in the kitchen. We, the daughters in the territory, received your parcel. Your parcel,

Mr Wassermann—

I left the kitchen and pulled on a hat in the hall. I could already hear the horse's hooves outside. In the station were only Officers Heller and Bussig, talking about Henrik's wife, the weaker sex, they said, that pinched sex of Henrik's wife. I put all the orchids I could find in a crate—Heribert Stein's protégés. Bussig blocked my way harshly, addressing me as Missy and laughing maliciously.

Watering, was all I said, picking up the orchids and escaping.

I walked the territory while Fritzi wrote to Peter Wassermann. The orchids swayed to and fro. The horse Bataille ate a bud, and I sang the song of the hammer out loud. The hammer of my mother, I sang.

That day will come!

One of the orchids I planted outside Elisabeth Korn's door, the others around the ventilation shaft. Then I leaned against the horse and shouted aloud:

Hey! Fritzi! I'm planting orchids in the ground here! What are you doing?

Fritzi was too far away to hear me of course, but I shouted on and sang the song of the hammer once more.

It was Officer Dünckel, patrolling the territory by night, who discovered the orchids by the ventilation shaft. After consulting the police commander he trampled the plants with his boots and then smoked a cigarette before getting back in his car. We happened to be sitting behind the ventilation shaft at the time, discussing astronomical matters.

F. Engels wrote, said Elisabeth Korn, about a river *between smoky factory buildings and yarn-strewn bleaching yards*, and the river, this river, was red, Engels wrote, crimson, he wrote, *due simply and solely to the numerous dye-works using Turkey red*.

According to a number of theories from the newspapers of the flying woodpecker, said Fritzi, we are currently in a state which is up for discussion, as a certain emptiness lies before us and, you understand, is veritably waiting for us to do something about it. A state long awaited by the writers of the flying woodpecker.

Then again, spoke Fritzi later with a frown, there are only very few of us, and the aforementioned certain emptiness is currently mainly laid claim to by

Heller's watch, the car, commodities and security,

obedience, composure,

the preservation of constant composure

of security

and the associated securing of property.

According to a number of these theories, said Fritzi, we are currently in an extremely difficult situation, as we have been unable all our lives, since our very births, to picture anything but the current situation of this territory. Personally, she said, I have never seen a woodpecker, for example, or a strike. Nor once the miners with their lamps. Since we thus have few points of reference and the relevant, possibly highly informative written matter (the chronicle, the letters, the reports, the biographies) is kept from us or dismissed as useless, said Fritzi, according to a number of theories we are currently in an extremely difficult situation.

A resolution was delivered to us.

Resolution:

In order to meet the growing need for security, the police in the territory will henceforth be supported by a
privately run company under the management of H.
Stein, by the name of: SEDISEST plc (Security and
District Service Stein).

The responsibilities of SEDISEST MANAGEMENT
and SECURITY include maintaining security, particularly including that of material assets in public and
private areas,

their protection from criminal and elemental damages,

the issuing and administration of official papers,

the maintenance of the borders,

identity checks,

the arrest, detention and reprimanding of criminal
offenders and/or suspicious persons.

We will focus our efforts on the trouble-free and
discreet exercising of our activity within your surround-

ings. Our employees are qualified by high personal responsibility and a healthy pride in their profession. Through their presence, SEDISEST SECURITY contributes to an improvement in general security.

Signed: H. Stein, Director and Chief of Front Operations

Fritzi to Dünckel, who is standing in the car park with Bussig:

We once again have a number of questions for Chief of Front Operations Stein, who is also our father.

But Stein is not on site,
Identity checks in dangerous places,
says Dünckel.

The landscape suddenly seems further, further and further away. It's the evening breaking, or it's this annoyance (Dünckel, SEDISEST SECURITY! Identity check) that's making my head go crazy.

It's making my head go crazy, I screamed in Dünckel's face. It can't be true! It's making me all thunderous and dumb! It's absolutely unbearable! And I tried to kick Dünckel in the shins with both feet.

And it really was that way: I sensed myself veritably losing my mind. It circled above me a while and my head grew quite empty and still. A magpie flew away with it.

I was still striking out at Dünckel, screaming to lose my mind. Didn't Fritzi wear a knife on her belt, was my last thought,

then I lay still and slept for long hours.

Once I heard my father at my bedside. In a calm voice, he spoke to me:

Margarete, we trust in our future. In values and skills. We're planning our goals with foresight, we're pursuing them doggedly. Security creates trust. Security protects us and our values.

In my sleep, it came to me: I had hit out at Dünckel with all my might. Had my mind then flown away on the back of a magpie?

Leave me alone, just let me sleep before rising again.

On 11 May many years ago, 7000 workers from the Good Courage Mine near Wildenstadt went on strike. Another 10,000 downed tools in Belkenburg, 4000 in Usten. There followed strikes in Hasseldorf, St Beinsen and Oberfeldstadt, strikes in all parts of the coal district.

Votes were held in the mines on further actions. Ninety-one delegations, elected by over 20,000 miners and employees, set out to announce the demands they had drawn up in the capital.

Fritzi roused me with the wakening call of the sea-farers:

Rise, rise!

five days before the winter.

Dried splashes of mud covered her skin in places. Her boots were dripping, and outside whinnied the horse Bataille. I instantly thought of the world's longest rivers, among them the Congo and the Huang He, fell back asleep with them, listening to the rattle in my chest. As if I were stumbling through mountainscapes rich in ravines.

Fritzi roused me with the wakening call of the seafarers five days before the winter. Then the two of us went out of the house and crossed the empty spaces, the former roads. Not a sound, only the horse's hooves behind us. At 6:30 this morning I found the sink-hole, said Fritzi suddenly as we walked. A tiny channel vanishing into it.

Behind us, the horse shied.

All the days that I waited and read.

I read at the kitchen table. While Fritzi roamed the territory, I read

long and anxiously on my journey southward.

And there it was, then there it was, it was here, it was a sinkhole. A tiny channel vanishing into it. We stood on the edge of a darkness, and it drew us into uncertainty. PONOR. We sat down. Do we have to wait until the channel swells to a stream, until the sinkhole can no longer hold all the water? I asked. Would that be the river?

A house stood to the left not far from the sinkhole. A burgundy carpet led up the staircase. In the dining hall hung a chandelier with no bulbs.

The long corridors of the Hotel Bellagio, Las Vegas. The corridors of Caesar's Palace, the corridors of the Mirage. Of the MGM Grand Hotel, of the Flamingo, Las Vegas, of the Treasure Island.

And the long corridors of the Circus Hotel in Reno, the corridors of the Eldorado Hotel in Reno, of Harrah's, of Tony Roma's, of the Best Western Airport Plaza Hotel.

Fritzi nodded. A hotel, four storeys, hot-water taps, power sockets, fuse boxes, bedrooms with no beds, bedrooms with bed frames, lamps, sockets for light bulbs, hotplates, storage rooms, fire extinguishers on all floors.

We sat talking for hours on two wooden chairs from Sacramento in the salon. I asked her about the knife I had suspected she wore on her belt. Fritzi nodded, yes.

Then she said, we must be aware that

the madness—

we must, she said, be aware that we can only ever speak of madness with relation to a reality—

that madness only exists in deviation from this reality. Thus, when we claim there is a reality—

we must therefore, yes, claim there is another reality. Then the magpies will circle above the heads of H. Stein and the watchmen and no longer above ours.

We immediately resolved: We shall take up residence in this house, we shall move out and settle here.

So we loaded everything we had into the car. Blankets, clothes and the books, the coffee machine and the coffee cups, a reading lamp, the typewriter, a crate of beer and that kind of thing.

On the way we stopped at the crossroads and stuck a note to the traffic light, which stood at an angle and did not work. It read: We have moved.

I sat on a stone with my back to the house. Fritzi shrugged on a coat and turned around as the first snow fell.

CHINA

The winter remains a blank line on the sheet of paper
I inserted into the typewriter.

But the horse is standing in the snow behind the hotel, drinking out of a trough. With the arrival of winter, greater peace entered our lives.

Where are all the snow geese?

Once a day we walk the few footsteps to the sinkhole and examine the tiny channel vanishing unwaveringly into the crater. If it keeps snowing, by the time the snow thaws a river will form, far exceeding what the sinkhole can hold.

Until then we wait, letting our gaze roam. In the distance an occasional SEDISEST car patrols. The task of the watchmen is to observe us as discreetly as possible but they do not know where we are. They comb the large territory and position observation posts but the daughters are not to be found and the horse Bataille is white on white.

We hibernate in the land of snow. The winter seems to stretch back several generations, it stretches far back in time. It is the winter before the summer of the birth of Buenaventura Durruti, and it is the winter in whose deep nights Rosa Stein was born and Rosa Luxemburg was killed. It is the same long winter, the winter before the awakening! the uprising!

we stand at the edge of a valley of snow, looking out over the plain, a hill, a grove, back at years of snow, back decades and across countless epochs of snow we look, out across the snow-covered rise, the ridge and the peaks, the lowland, the middle ground. Down through the great valley of snow we descend, into the ravine across the slopes, across the hillsides down the hillsides. We see the gulf, the gorge, the snow on the square outside the house where we once lived, now covering the cars too.

The winter is here at the moment but the snowfall will soon lighten. The only measure against freezing to death for now is climbing over the hill of snow.

On the other side of the hill of snow is the old printing plant. Fritzi and the horse have broken a narrow path there, and on skis, on slats and old boards we now drag the duplication machines through the snow over the hill or around the hill. We have tied a rope around the horse Bataille's belly too, our fingers clammy.

Fritzi cries a birdcall into the air just before the highest point of the hill.

The duplication machines slip sideways away from us on the slats, leaving traces of oil in the snow until we catch them at the last moment with our red hands.

Fritzi is lying in the snow.

There are only two of us but we do have a horse, she says, exhausted.

Then she begins to laugh and laughs on and on, as the horse and I drag the machines the last few metres across the snow and then take our daily walk to the sinkhole, and once we get back Fritzi's not laughing any more of course.

There are in fact only two of us (and one horse), I write that evening but I can now say with certainty that there are more of us. Here are those too whom we remember, and those for whom we have resolved to wait. When Fritzi laughed today in the snow, perhaps she was thinking of turning a corner on a bicycle and just before that calling to the remembered and the awaited over her shoulder:

We'll meet this evening by the river!

Don't forget: this evening!

Meet by the river!

This evening we'll sit by the river!

See you by the river!

We'll see each other on the riverbank!

Bring cake!

Bring sausages for everyone!

Put on a warm sweater or a windbreaker!

Come riding on your bicycles!

Come mounted on your white horses!

I too once thought myself alone in this land.

Ernst Thal came to the hotel, just in time before the great snowstorm. He brought Bruckner's *Pains of Youth*, laid it on the counter in the lobby. He gave the duplication machines a brief examining stroke of his hands. He chose a room on the third floor and has since mainly slept, when he's not walking to the sink-hole with us.

At the sinkhole of the Buenaventura, we make plans for the time after the long winter. Plans to remedy (a) our pitiful existence and (b) this pitifully wasted stretch of land.

We plan a conference that shall culminate in a great celebration. We shall undertake a trip on the Bue-naventura in a wooden rowing boat which shall take us all the way to China. We shall proclaim the land anew. We shall ride in circles on Bataille and then suddenly veer off and disappear. We shall perform Bruckner's *Pains of Youth* in numerous languages but we shall not put on costumes. We shall invite countless guests, among them many mining scientists, lady archaeologists, a squad of firemen, lady and gentle-man representatives of the arts, the miners of all con-tinents, a typographer, a number of young people, bold of heart.

A hotel awaits you, I write in the official invitation. Ernst Thal nods. Accommodation will be provided, I write. You may stay in the hotel, I write.

I type letter after letter: the great celebration! of the re-discovery of the River Buenaventura! And I insert each one into an envelope.

To the Academy of Mining Science

To a band from London that we heard on the radio

To the aforementioned typographer

To Ms Erika Gerste and Messirs Hirsch and Elm

To a geography student from Berlin and Freudenberg

To a surveyor from the former GDR

To the firemen of New York

To a number of hobos from Idaho, Kansas and Montana

To Norma Jackson, lady archaeologist

To the lady photographer and war reporter who studied in Frankfurt am Main

To the poets Wassermann, Leu and Becker

To the lady chroniclers of the northern lands of Africa

To the first deputy mayor of Reykjavik

To the youth of Athens

Then we send off the letters, for which we have to take one last long drive this winter. We make coffee and pour it into thermos flasks and set off. *Pains of Youth* is still in the lobby. Fritzi nods wearily out to the morning, and Ernst Thal sits quietly on the back seat. We shiver and drink coffee and spill half of it as we suddenly cross unexpected railway tracks. We drive through the morning, sleepy and calm. It's our home for the moment, as if we had just cast anchor and the harbour walls had just vanished in the mist and the ocean we were sailing lay ahead of us again. As if we were standing on the bridge, confident and drinking coffee out of thermos flasks.

The letters are safe on the back seat with Ernst Thal.

It is a kind of border checkpoint where I stop the car, almost vanished in the snow. It is a small construction trailer with two windows and a barrier next door, always pointing in the same direction: straight across the road. Here sits a border guard with a grim expression and suspicious eyes, says Fritzi, he is armed and responsible for fending off forced entry to the restricted zone, primarily on the part of tourists and traders. Fritzi and Ernst Thal climb the three steps and knock at the door, hand him the letters, insistently, hand him money for the postage stamps, put the change back in their pockets. They speak to him. I don't understand a word.

Now everything's in his hands for the moment, I say with concern. Fritzi says: Margarete, you're not forgetting you're a grown woman, are you? Keep your emotions in check. Ernst Thal laughs in his sleep. If the border guard doesn't send off the letters, we'll come back and shoot him, says Fritzi. I laugh.

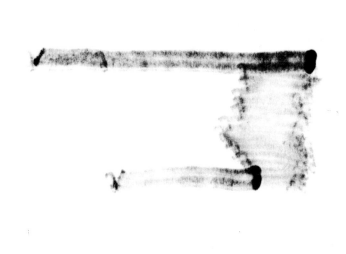

ACKNOWLEDGEMENTS

This texts quotes freely from Thomas Hart Benton, John Bidwell, Ferdinand Bruckner, Buddha, Joseph Conrad, David DeKok, W. H. Emory, Friedrich Engels, John Charles Frémont, Erich Fromm, Godspeed You! Black Emperor, Johann Wolfgang von Goethe, Hanns Günther, George Jackson, Deryl B. Johnson, Joseph Nicolas Nicollet, Robert Walser, Peter Wassermann, Johann David Wyss, Émile Zola and from articles in the *Brockhaus ABC der Naturwissenschaft und Technik*.